Blank Check

poems by

Kathi Stafford

Finishing Line Press
Georgetown, Kentucky

Blank Check

Copyright © 2016 by Kathi Stafford
ISBN 978-1-944251-68-0 First Edition
All rights reserved under International and Pan-American Copyright Conventions. No part of this book may be reproduced in any manner whatsoever without written permission from the publisher, except in the case of brief quotations embodied in critical articles and reviews.

ACKNOWLEDGMENTS

Editor: Christen Kincaid

Cover Art: Kathi Stafford

Author Photo: Kathi Stafford

Cover Design: Elizabeth Maines

Printed in the USA on acid-free paper.
Order online: www.finishinglinepress.com
also available on amazon.com

> Author inquiries and mail orders:
> Finishing Line Press
> P. O. Box 1626
> Georgetown, Kentucky 40324
> U. S. A.

Table of Contents

What There Was to See 1

Division 2

Blank Check 3

Bound 5

All sorrows will heal 6

In West Texas, we would have called him a character 7

These Bones 8

The Conversation 9

Recurrence 10

Musings on the Afterlife during Chemo 11

Remember, remember 12

Man of Bavaria 14

My talisman 15

Cancer Train 16

Island warning for the traveler 17

Like a Gliding 18

Communion 19

Cyclone over Chennai 20

All pearls are tears 21

Palms 22

For my husband, Daniel William Martin

What There Was to See

After we bowed down to the Corots
And acknowledge our debt   and after
We saw the starry night and its comet

Tails and as soon as we murmured
Beneath the wheat fields and analyzed
Each brush stroke of Van Gogh

We sat down to tea beneath the palms
Next to the fountain   that erratic source
Of spare coins and cool water

We paled in peach linen and applied balm
To our over-chemoed souls   cut out
Percussion and thrill

Drank rough earl grey and played
With the lavender cloth that pulled
Beneath the china lips

Pulled together against memory
And rested a bit   and pretended we were girls
From a sketch in that museum

Unscarred   blank   sighing

Division

We used to hold
hands near the bower. Now, we lean together,
quiet, and that is enough.

Evening came fast—too dark to look
for avocados any more. The sprawling
tree filled the yard, its branches large
and smoky brown. A tangy scent
floats at dusk as honeysuckle
 trims along the fence.

Perhaps my cells split
sideways as I sat on the bench
in the silence. I asked him to pick the
fruit, but the hour was late. A woman light
on her path keeps moving anyway.

Blank Check

One year ago today: my first go
at radiation. The tech with his arms
full of blue tattoos and scars eases me
into place. The quiet clicking

Machine drones on as I hold still
in its shadow. A thin red light razors
below my skin, down into an ocean
of cells and fear. In a few weeks, my skin will

Come off—each strip delicate
and lacy. So individual, each layer
with its sheer story of my past. Some women
are stronger than I am.

Thirty-three times I go home after and fall
into sleep, so hard and final.

I win the lottery. One year come
and gone
with no new lumps. This is a gift
and a wonder to me. Will there always be
a blank check made out
to future scars?

Maybe I never ask the right questions.
There's a tale for every traveler.

The tech guy talks on about his newborn,
Jimmy, three months old, while he shines
with joy. He's trying to distract me. I know.

I lie still and
take it all in.

My pain held up on all four corners
by the prayers lifted by my saints, my friends, towards
gentle sky, oh Metta, oh peace of my soul.

Bound

I drink from the bitter well of the breast. Milk twirls down
Into every space: clavicle, ulna, femur. Pushes apart
Atoms until blank goes the canvas. A raw growth begins.

I am bound up, crippled
With judgment. The girl who tells everyone
Just what to do. At my desk, I hear Rome,
Shelley, Iliad. Haystacks stagger along the horizon.

My box of rules, scraped and narrow.
Me   hung up to dry
Like a curing deer under a Texas sunset
Boiling with clouds and snakes.
I watch me   separate   unconnected:
No self, no truth.

Take a hammer to those rules.
Now come instead,
Grace, oh sweet milk;
Joy, oh sweet ocean.

All sorrows will heal

A trail marked with incense and myrrh. Daily trips
To radiation, a drive to the oncologist, the rub of lotion
Into scars. A nurse slips me a cookie. Another
Touches my shoulder, just for a moment.

A friend is on the phone, asks if I could manage
Some tomato soup today. A girl I hardly know, Sarah,
Sends a little note each week.

I told everyone I would do it myself
And I didn't want help or pity. But this net of strength
Bound me on days I could not move.

All sorrows will heal. Wait for eternity
To fill one's eyes and hands.

In West Texas, we would have called him a character

Bruce   minor reality TV star
Bodybuilder   my sort of friend for ten years

Rolled his car in the Arizona desert, walked five miles,
And died the day of my first surgery. No one knows where
The two dogs went.   I know he had a sweet
Tooth for cards and poker games, a man with three

Ex-wives, a son who failed him, and wads of cash
He stashed here and there. He told me once *I like vodka
Too much*. In West Texas, we would have called him a character.
Tried to go Buddhist but was an altar
Boy at heart. I'd like to find the cause of death.

Sometimes he'd fake an accent when he's call me and say
This is Colonel Klingon or something else ridiculous. I hung up
On the man a lot. He laughed so hard at his own jokes. Yet I hope

When he walked his last five miles he finally
Found that spot between sacraments and rites he needed,
A place full of movement
With joy in his present steps.

How he prided himself. The shadow man, gone to ground
Outside Phoenix in a beige landscape where the
Temple people knew his name, Bruce.

These Bones

The hieroglyphic code from these bones
puts on a shadow play. Ulna turns to dust
Within my body. When will the crest of pain

Die down, recede on the pebbled edge
Of the tributary?

Oh my bones. How I took you for granted,
Never bearing my full weight in the whirl

Along the banks of the Paria River. I pray
Mercy for cartilage   sinew   nerves

In the shadow of Bryce Canyon.

The Conversation

The lymph nodes send their secret through the
trails of my body. The gadgets, injected, make their
Radioactive way through the veins, seeking out
Damage (or conversely, a bit of good news for a change).

I spark up a conversation with the technician, his Slavic accent
Pure and dashing while he flirts with me, a secondhand
And sewn up mess.

All finished, he says, "Sadly, our encounter
Here now ends," and touches my shoulder with a gentle
Pat. A pictograph of my undone cells is all I have left of his
Long black hair and sardonic wink.

Recurrence

The verdict came at me sideways   malignant

Never the word one wants to hear   gauze still clinging

From the biopsy   in short

The cobblestone of my breast   my lung

Short-changed and dotted   unspoiled

Now dreary   I stipulate

I've had a good life   no pre-printed

Program for me   was there?

Musings on the Afterlife during Chemo

He wonders if he and Mom will have Sunday dinner

Together again, like the used to at Sam's Café

Over on Oak Street. With the faded white curtains

And the tough beef neither of them could manage too well

What with their bad teeth and all. Weak sun would waver

Its way to their coffee cups, hers with its lipstick kisses

Vibrant and blue red. As the cords coil up around

His bed, like asps waiting for a final goodnight nip, he hopes that

The brisket will be better in heaven, that they will only play Stevie Ray

Vaughn on the weekends, and that Mom will finally hear him out just this once.

Remember, remember

My mother's pillbox hat
Just like Jackie O's
Powder blue with a peach trim

Scalloped edges worn with white
Gloves only on Sundays
Every stitch precise

Back to the story of camels
Told in a story box filled with sand
As my lungs were bound by secret spells

Remember the greats
Pampa   Grandpa Hart
Pa Hestand   Gramma Stafford

Her gray hair spilled to the waist
Even at seventy   pride
Of the family   braided or loose

So many pieces sewn up in me last
Year   my friend asked what
Could be left in me by now   who knows

Who gave me these odd cells
Teeming   that have to go
What stories came with the mitochondria

The edges of estrogen and lime
That one hopes are gone forever
Without knowing for sure

Wearing that hat against the
Uncertainty   those braids against
Certain loss and the indifference of the

Oklahoma prairie to whatever is left
Behind from the pioneer bond
The ancients carried within them

Man of Bavaria

Glitter falls out of my hem
Where the tailor tucked it in

With his love potion   a secret mix
A powder of unknown dimensions

My husband is suspicious
Why does that man beam

When you walk into
His shop of thread?

He takes up my slack
Edges and only says

*It will keep your illness
Missing—in remission, no?*

He is pulling for me in his dusty
Shop on Wilshire   he knows

My chemo pill tricks
Counting backwards

Ten to one while my haunted body

Radiates in the taut heat of a blue dress

Dan grows jealous
The tailor smiles

Wide and hungry
Is my shrinking self
That still fights invisibility

My talisman

The red book   all embroidery
and gold sequins   on its front
where I scribble   my little memories
and dreams   of five months in India.

Bangalore   where I hiked
and prayed   alone for so long
but not alone either   in contradiction
the banyan tree   its twisting bark
turning into roads   that I hike between villages
while unknown cells   sprang up
watery and silent   waiting to be revealed.

The pages   filled up now
with words   I learned in Hindi
my recognized language   from the roots of a yellow
bush outside   swerve of my balcony's drop.

Cancer Train

I had a ticket in my breast   didn't choose it
But it showed the track I was bound to take

Here the whistle blows as the train goes
Through the desert   then the valley filled with pines

Next to the chest lay the node
The surgeon went deep to find it

I know it's coming back   says one friend
About her trials

Yes sister
sing those blues

Yet will I find a way
To hold that slow growth way within me
To lay it down and ring it out and
Sing to victory

Island warning for the traveler

On the surface the air is clear and the birds seem so placid and satisfied by the fresh cold breeze. But underneath the surface lay cells made of ice and tunnels. Step the wrong way on the surface and you'll slide right under into the maze with no escape. The slimy walls will break your wails right down to nothing. Penguins freeze to death in ten seconds at that depth. You thought you'd fly right back off this spot from the island airport, soar over the sour earth and pockets of rust along the tundra verge. It's harder to leave this Arctic lawn than one might think. So take your steps with care. Watch out for the neighbor and his oxygen tank. Any day blood could slow right down, forget to flow through vein and artery, ice over in a purple dawn.

Like a Gliding

" …where a forest fire spread
Looking like a gliding
Golden rope
With which the rich
Tie their elephants …"
   Odhlanthaiyar

The growth starts in my chest deep in South
India. Strong as a chord that ties up wild
Beasts. An impatient elephant
Slings his trunk against the wall.

But without energy.
He's tried that game before,
At holiday. The children

Will be hoisted to his back
First. Lentils boil
In the kitchen's rapid heat

Waiting for the curry kiss.
He'll bear the burden
Across his mottled skin.

Festival in the village. Think
Too much about the animal's point
Of view. The tumor grows. A forest fire burns

Beneath paper ears. Trample
Down the red path
Deep in his silent name.

Communion

I went out of my way for the ocean. I wanted
Just a quick look at the waves, a smell of sand away
From the refinery glare. Made lots of wrong turns,
Got fed up, almost retraced my path.

Sea wasn't there. Well, of course it was there, but low
Hills and pink condos blocked the view I might
Have seen. Salt hung heavy in my mouth,
Communion with the unseen.

Went out of my way to take the chemo
Pills and all my lumps with a good attitude. Diagnosed
But waiting for results. Plotted my destination through
Fog. I didn't see everything.

I'll find the right path now. Pull to the
Shoulder, wait for the block of waves to wash over
El Segundo, believe I was made to see this view,
To watch the moon rest on the waves of the moment.

Cyclone over Chennai

Cyclone over Chennai
Dragging its dirty tail
Down low. Spatters

Its rainy thoughts
Along the coast.
South tip of India

Takes its bath
Like a good child.
Spinning up,

The layered wash
Hits hard. Like the edge
That walloped me fast when

Cancer came to me; India as
Well. I didn't choose either home:
Work for the flight, fate for the growth.

The paths we walked down. Dark red earth,
Fields in the hills outside Belur, where peacocks
Cry in the banyan trees. Learn to

Push through, make it home. Know
That all will come to rest, sweet
Child still there, patient and ready.

All pearls are tears

The feel of pearls	cold and dead
Hard against my neck	*Please help me, dear*
A clasp I cannot	pink and off white
From ocean floors	I run my fingers along
This strand	while the blue truck bounces
In front of me	down Lincoln gone south
The trunk bears	hibiscus: snow blooms
Escape the trellis	smell of pavement
I finger each bead	its pollen long a part of me
What I gave up	for image
While far below	a basement filled with
Stumps of long	gone elms and a shorn girl
Come gentle sky	bring together lost limbs
The needy catch	is it necklace or chain
Peals hit the ground	while jazz plays slow
Thread up all	and sew them up fast

Palms

I turned pages in my
Book—each page blank,
Forlorn.　　　Empty.

I wake up and walk
To my radiation round.
Light filters down

Through the palms
On my way to the bed of
Sorrow.　But just now, hot

California sun bounces off
My hands.　I turn into the office, as
Angelita grabs my shoulder and

Gives me a pat.　Time for Psalms
Now. For my gloom to light up
And match the crooked light

Coming in the window slats. To breathe in
All healing. To remember the one who suffered
Before me　　and far beyond me.

My foundation who saw the grave
Beauty of the world.　Who touched
Every wound.

Kathi Stafford's poetry, articles, and interviews have appeared in *Rattle, Chiron Review, Connecticut River Review,* and numerous other literary journals. Her poetry has appeared in numerous anthologies, such as *Chopin with Cherries* and *Hitchcock Review.* She previously served as Poetry Editor and Senior Editor for *Southern California Review* for several years.